FOREWORD

   After completing this project, I am further convinced that arranging can be as challenging, exhausting, and rewarding as composing original music.

   Every hymn, spiritual, and spiritual song in this collection was arranged lovingly and meticulously, but only after listening and only after experiencing the uniqueness of line, harmonies, and substance. Above all else, each had to be a good fit within the duet experience.

   Find a friend and enjoy these duets. I took special care to ensure that melody was shared in both parts, harmonies or countermelodies were interesting and unique, and overall effect would be enjoyed by any listener.

Kenneth D. Friedrich

INDEX

cont.

A Mighty Fortress Is Our God

Ein' Feste Burg

Martin Luther
Kenneth D. Friedrich

A Mighty Fortress

Abide With Me

"Eventide' by William Henry Monk
Kenneth D. Friedrich

All Hail the Power of Jesus' Name

Oliver Holden (1765-1844)
Kenneth D. Friedrich

All Hail the Power of Jesus' Name

All Things Bright and Beautiful

English melody, 17th century
Kenneth D. Friedrich

All Things Bright and Beautiful

Amazing Grace

Traditonal American melody
Kenneth D. Friedrich

Amazing Grace

America, the Beautiful

Samuel A. Ward (1882)
Kenneth D. Friedrich

America The Beautiful

Are You Washed

Elisha A. Hoffman (1839-1929)
Kenneth D. Friedrich

Battle Hymn of the Republic

American Camp Meeting Tune
Kenneth D. Friedrich

Battle Hymn of the Republic

Be Still, My Soul

Jean Sibelius
Kenneth D. Friedrich

Be Still, My Soul

Be Thou My Vision

Old Irish Folk Tune
Kenneth D. Friedrich

Be Thou My Vision

Blessed Assurance

Phoebe Palmer Knapp (1839-1908)
Kenneth D. Friedrich

Blessed Be The Name

Anonymous
Kenneth D. Friedrich

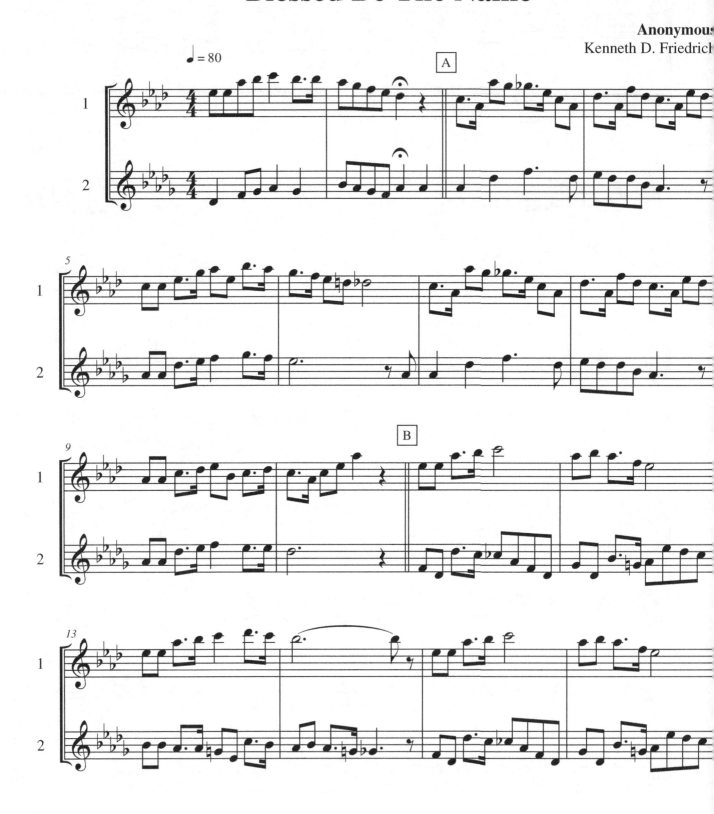

Blessed Be The Name

Blest Be the Tie That Binds

Johann G. Nageli (1773-1836)
Kenneth D. Friedrich

Come, Thou Fount of Every Blessing

Anonymous
Kenneth D. Friedrich

Come, Ye Thankful People, Come

George J. Elvey (1816-1893)
Kenneth D. Friedrich

Crown Him With Many Crowns

George J. Elvey (1816-1893
Kenneth D. Friedrich

Crown Him With Many Crowns

Eternal Father, Strong to Save

John B. Dykes (1823-1876)
Kenneth D. Friedrich

Fairest Lord Jesus

Richard Storrs Willis (1819-1900)
Kenneth D. Friedrich

Faith of Our Fathers

Henri F. Hemy
Kenneth D. Friedrich

Faith of Our Fathers

For the Beauty of the Earth

Conrad Kocher (1786-1872

Kenneth D. Friedrich

Glorious Things of Thee Are Spoken

Franz Joseph Haydn
Kenneth D. Friedrich

Glorious Things of Thee Are Spoken

God of Our Fathers

George W. Warren (1828-1902)
Kenneth D. Friedrich

God of Our Fathers

Great Is Thy Faithfulness

William M. Runyan (1870-1957)
Kenneth D. Friedrich

Hail to the Lord's Anointed

English melody
Kenneth D. Friedrich

Hail to the Lord's Anointed

Have Thine Own Way, Lord

George C. Stebbins (1846-1945)
Kenneth D. Friedrich

Have Thine Own Way, Lord

He Is Lord

Traditional
Kenneth D. Friedrich

He Leadeth Me

William B. Bradbury
Kenneth D. Friedrich

He Lives

Alfred H. Ackley (1887-196(
Kenneth D. Friedric

Here I Am, Lord

Daniel L. Schutte
Kenneth D. Friedrich

58

Here I Am, Lord

His Name Is Wonderful

Audrey Mieir (1916-1991

Kenneth D. Friedric

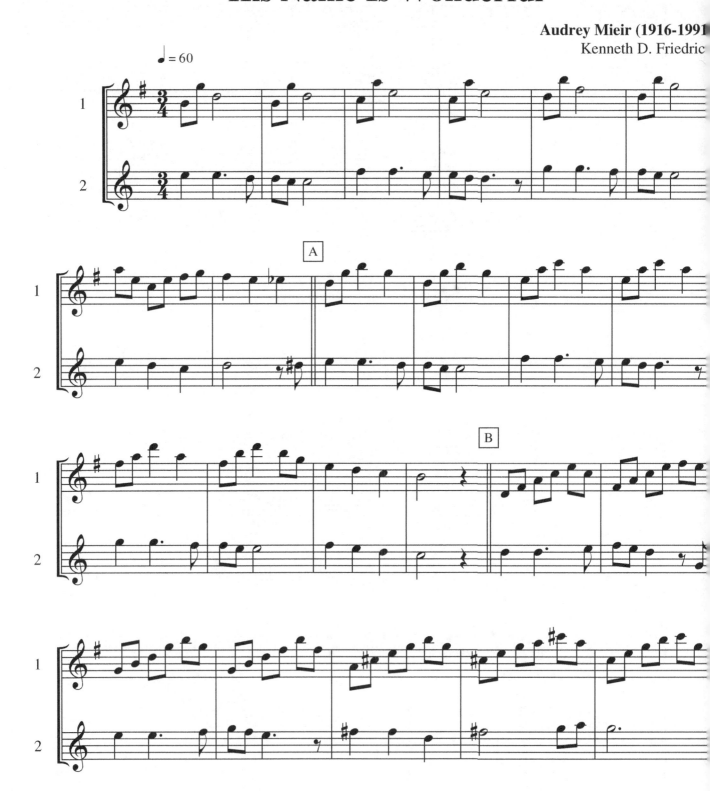

Holy, Holy, Holy

Reginald Heber
Kenneth D. Friedrich

Holy, Holy, Holy

How Great Thou Art

Swedish Folk Melody
Kenneth D. Friedrich

I Have Decided

Indian Folk Song
Kenneth D. Friedrich

I Have Decided

I Know That My Redeemer Liveth

James H. Fillmore (1849-1930
Kenneth D. Friedric

I Know That My Redeemer Liveth

I Love to Tell the Story

William G. Fisher
Kenneth D. Friedrich

I Love to Tell the Story

I Love You, Lord

Laurie Klei
Kenneth D. Friedric

I Love You, Lord

I Need Thee Every Hour

Robert Lowry (1826-1899)
Kenneth D. Friedrich

I Need Thee Every Hour

I Sing the Mighty Power of God

Gesangbuch der Herzogl (178
Kenneth D. Friedric

I Sing the Mighty Power of God

I Surrender All

Winfield S. Weeden (1847-1908)
Kenneth D. Friedrich

I Surrender All

If You Will Only Let God Guide You

Georg Neumark (1621-1681

Kenneth D. Friedric

If You Will Only Let God Guide You

Immortal, Invisible, God Only Wise

Traditional Welsh Hymn Melody
Kenneth D. Friedrich

Immortal, Invisible, God Only Wise

In the Garden

C. Austin Miles (1868-194€

Kenneth D. Friedric

84

In the Garden

I've Got Peace Like a River

Negro Spiritual
Kenneth D. Friedrich

I've Got Peace Like a River

Jesus Loves Me

William B. Bradbury (1816-186?
Kenneth D. Friedric

Jesus Loves Me

Jesus, Lover of My Soul

Joseph Parry
Kenneth D. Friedrich

Jesus, Lover of My Soul

Joyful, Joyful, We Adore Thee

Ludwig V. Beethoven
Kenneth D. Friedrich

Joyful, Joyful, We Adore Thee

Just As I Am

William B. Bradbury
Kenneth D. Friedrich

Just As I Am

Lead On, O King Eternal

Henry T. Smart (1813-187?)

Kenneth D. Friedric

Leaning on the Everlasting Arms

Anthony J. Showalter (1858-1924)
Kenneth D. Friedrich

Leaning on the Everlasting Arms

Let Us Break Bread Together

Traditional Spiritu.
Kenneth D. Friedri

Let Us Break Bread Together

rit.

rit.

Lift Up Your Heads

Thomas Williams' Psalmodia Evan
Kenneth D. Friedrich

Lift Up Your Heads

O For a Thousand Tongues to Sing

Carl G. Glaser (1784-182
Kenneth D. Friedri

O For a Thousand Tongues to Sing

104

(The) Lily of the Valley

William S. Hayes (1837-1907)
Kenneth D. Friedrich

(The) Lily of the Valley

Love Divine, All Loves Excelling

William Penfro Rowlands (1860
Kenneth D. Friedri

Love Divine, All Loves Excelling

Morning Has Broken
(Bunessan)

Traditional Gaelic Melody
Kenneth D. Friedrich

Morning Has Broken

My Faith Looks Up To Thee

Lowell Mason (1808-186
Kenneth D. Friedric

My Faith Looks Up To Thee

The Solid Rock

William B. Bradbury (1816-1868)
Kenneth D. Friedrich

The Solid Rock

My Tribute

Andrae Crouch (1942-201
Kenneth D. Friedri

My Tribute

Nearer, My God, To Thee

Lowell Mason
Kenneth D. Friedrich

Nearer, My God, To Thee

Now Thank We All Our God

Johann Cruger (1595-166
arr. by Kenneth D. Friedric

O Lord, Hear My Prayer

Jacques Berthier
Kenneth D. Friedrich

O Lord, Hear My Prayer

O Love, How Deep

Adapted by Michael Praetorius
Kenneth D. Friedrich

O Love, How Deep

O Master, Let Me Walk With Thee

Percy Smith (1825-1898)
Kenneth D. Friedrich

O Perfect Love

Joseph Barnl
Kenneth D. Friedri

O Perfect Love

O Sons and Daughters, Let Us Sing

French melody (18th Century)
Kenneth D. Friedrich

O Sons and Daughters, Let Us Sing

Meno Mosso

O Worship the King

Johann Michael Haydn (1737-18
Kenneth D. Friedric

O Worship the King

O, How I Love Jesus

American Melody
Kenneth D. Friedrich

O, How I Love Jesus

Of the Father's Love Begotten

13th Century Plainsong
Kenneth D. Friedrich

Of the Father's Love Begotten

Old Rugged Cross

George Bennard
Kenneth D. Friedrich

Old Rugged Cross

Onward, Christian Soldiers

Arthur S. Sullivan (1842-190
Kenneth D. Friedri

Parting Hymn

Edward J. Hopkins
Kenneth D. Friedrich

Parting Hymn

Praise God From Whom All Blessings Flow

Attributed to Louis Bourgeoi
Kenneth D. Friedri

Praise God From Whom All Blessings Flow

Praise to the Lord, the Almighty

Straisund Gesangbuch, 1665
Kenneth D. Friedrich

Praise to the Lord, the Almighty

Praise, My Soul, the King of Heaven

John Go
Kenneth D. Friedri

Praise, My Soul, the King of Heaven

Precious Lord, Take My Hand

Thomas A. Dorsey
Kenneth D. Friedrich

Precious Lord, Take My Hand

Rejoice, the Lord Is King

John Darwall (1731-178
Kenneth D. Friedri

Rejoice, the Lord Is King

Rejoice, Ye Pure in Heart

Arthur H. Messiter (1834-1916)
Kenneth D. Friedrich

Rejoice, Ye Pure in Heart

Rock of Ages

Thomas Hastings (1784-187
Kenneth D. Friedri

Rock of Ages

Savior, Like a Shepherd Lead Us

William B. Bradbury
Kenneth D. Friedrich

Savior, Like a Shepherd Lead Us

Seek Ye First

Karen Laffer
Kenneth D. Friedri

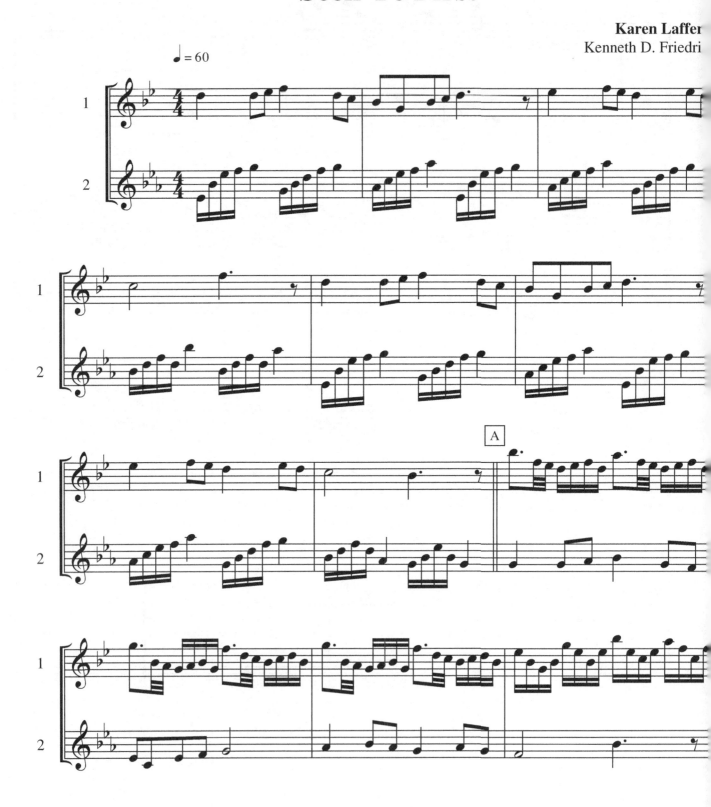

Shall We Gather at the River

Robert Lowry (1826-1899)
Kenneth D. Friedrich

Shall We Gather at the River

Softly and Tenderly

Will L. Thompson (1847-190
Kenneth D. Friedri

164

Softly and Tenderly

Soon and Very Soon

Andrae Crouch (1942-2015)
Kenneth D. Friedrich

Soon and Very Soon

Spirit of God, Descend Upon My Heart

Frederick C. Atkinson (1841-189[
Kenneth D. Friedri[

Spirit of God, Descend Upon My Heart

Spirit of the Living God

Daniel Iverson
Kenneth D. Friedrich

Stand Up, Stand Up for Jesus

George J. We
Kenneth D. Friedri

Stand Up, Stand Up for Jesus

Take My Life, and Let It Be Consecrated

Henri Malan
Kenneth D. Friedrich

Take My Life, and Let It Be Consecrated

The Joy of the Lord

Alliene G. Va
Kenneth D. Friedri

The Joy of the Lord

The King of Love My Shepherd Is

Traditional Irish Tune
Kenneth D. Friedrich

The King of Love My Shepherd Is

The Lord's Prayer

Swee Hong L
Kenneth D. Friedr

There Is A Balm in Gilead

African American Spiritual
Kenneth D. Friedrich

There Is A Balm in Gilead

There Is A Fountain

Early American Melo
Kenneth D. Friedri

There Is A Fountain

This Is My Father's World

Franklin L. Sheppard
Kenneth D. Friedrich

This Is My Father's World

Meno Mosso alla Grandioso

This Is the Day

Les Garr
Kenneth D. Friedri

This Is the Day

To God Be the Glory

George Washington Doane (1799-1859)
Kenneth D. Friedrich

To God Be the Glory

Trust and Obey

Daniel B. Towner (1850-191
Kenneth D. Friedri

192

Trust and Obey

We Gather Together

Adrianus Valerius's
Nederlandtsch Gedenckclanck
Kenneth D. Friedrich

Were You There?

African-American Spiritu
Kenneth D. Friedri

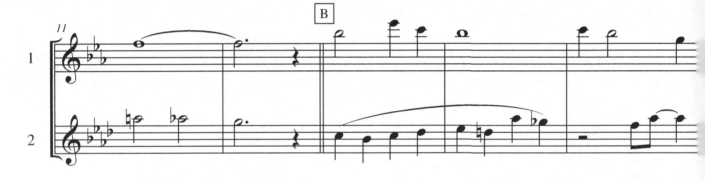

Were You There?

What a Friend We Have in Jesus

Charles A. Converse
Kenneth D. Friedrich

What Wondrous Love Is This

William Walker, *The Southern Harmony,* **18**
Kenneth D. Friedri

What Wondrous Love Is This

When the Roll Is Called Up Yonder

James M. Black (1856-1938)
Kenneth D. Friedrich

When the Roll Is Called Up Yonder

Made in the USA
Las Vegas, NV
02 October 2023

78475794R00116